HULL TRAMWAYS

Paul Morfitt
Malcolm Wells

Series editor Robert J Harley

MP Middleton Press

Cover picture: It is June 1938 and tram 130, dating from 1909 but much rebuilt, is passing the Beverley Road Baths on its way to the city centre. Other than a huge increase in traffic the scene is much the same today.

Cover colours: The livery of the trams was Crimson Lake and White.

Published June 2005

ISBN 1 904474 60 8

© Middleton Press, 2005

Design Deborah Esher

Published by
>   *Middleton Press*
>   *Easebourne Lane*
>   *Midhurst, West Sussex*
>   *GU29 9AZ*

Tel: 01730 813169
Fax: 01730 812601
Email: info@middletonpress.co.uk
www.middletonpress.co.uk

Printed & bound by Biddles Ltd, Kings Lynn

INDEX

1	Anlaby Road	50	Hedon Road
10	Hessle Road	55	Pier
16	Spring Bank	58	City Centre
20	Princes Avenue	81	Finale
26	Queens Road	84	Rolling Stock
27	Newland Avenue	106	Depots and Workshops
30	Cottingham Road	118	Leeds Service
35	Beverley Road	120	Preservation
45	Holderness Road		

INTRODUCTON AND ACKNOWLEDGEMENTS

There is, as yet, no definitive history of tramway operation in Kingston upon Hull although G A Lee's thesis of 1968 comes close. R J Buckley, C Dyson and G A Lee have described horse and steam days whilst Mick Nicholson and N Proudlock have outlined the signalling arrangements at level crossings. Another good read is Rod Berrieman's description of the Stoneferry saga.

This book does not attempt to be definitive but tries to portray the many moods of tramway operation within the city. Several photographs have appeared in print previously for it has proved difficult to obtain photographs of certain parts of the system, particularly Spring Bank West and Chanterlands Avenue. We have had to exercise great care with photographs since some bear a totally incorrect date and, occasionally, a wrong location. All come from our own collections or from fellow enthusiasts. We would also like to thank Mick Nicholson, the Hull Daily Mail and staff of the Local History Library in Hull.

Neither author is old enough to remember trams so they have placed much reliance on published sources of varying accuracy and books supplemented by recent research.

Outwardly, Hull's tramways seemed prosperous but professional and political rivalries often ensured that trams did not always attain their full potential.

GEOGRAPHICAL SETTING

The city of Kingston upon Hull lies on the north bank of the River Humber, some fifty-five miles (88.5 km) east of Leeds. It is bisected on the eastern edge of the city centre, by the River Hull which was spanned by two opening bridges, North Bridge and Drypool Bridge. Until 1932 there was a third, Monument Bridge, located between Queens Dock and Princes Dock which was removed when Queens Dock was filled in.

A frequent ferry service operated between the Corporation Pier, in the Old Town, and New Holland on the southern bank of the Humber. From here trains carried large numbers of passengers to Grimsby and Cleethorpes (especially in Summer).

Hull possessed no hills or gradients of any note and the flat, straight main roads facilitated not only the development of horse trams but also ensured that competing horse-drawn omnibuses and wagonettes lasted much longer than in comparable towns.

The city's population grew from 152,240 in 1881 to 204,259 in 1901, due in part to boundary extensions and by 1930 over 300,000 resided in the city.

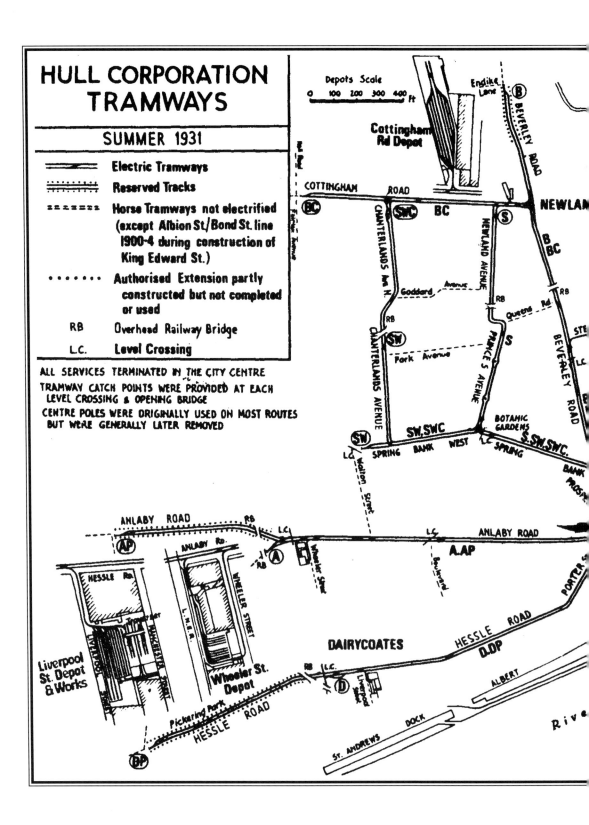

HULL CORPORATION TRAMWAYS

SUMMER 1931

Depots Scale

0 100 200 300 400 ft

Electric Tramways	
Reserved Tracks	
Horse Tramways not electrified (except Albion St./Bond St. line 1900-4 during construction of King Edward St.)	
Authorised Extension partly constructed but not completed or used	
RB	Overhead Railway Bridge
L.C.	Level Crossing

ALL SERVICES TERMINATED IN THE CITY CENTRE
TRAMWAY CATCH POINTS WERE PROVIDED AT EACH
LEVEL CROSSING & OPENING BRIDGE
CENTRE POLES WERE ORIGINALLY USED ON MOST ROUTES
BUT WERE GENERALLY LATER REMOVED

Cottingham Rd Depot

COTTINGHAM ROAD

NEWLAN...

Englike Lane

BEVERLEY ROAD

CHANTERLANDS Ave N.

NEWLAND AVENUE

Goddard Avenue

Queens Rd

BEVERLEY ROAD

STE...

CHANTERLANDS AVENUE

Park Avenue

PRINCES AVENUE

BOTANIC GARDENS

SW, SWC

SPRING BANK WEST

SPRING

S. SW. SWC.

BANK

Walton Street

ANLABY ROAD

RB

LC

Wheeler Street

ANLABY ROAD

A.AP

ANLABY Rd

WHEELER STREET

Boulevard

PORTER S...

HESSLE Rd

LMER

HESSLE ROAD

D.DP

Liverpool St. Depot & Works

Wheeler St. Depot

DAIRYCOATES

ALBERT

Pickering Park

HESSLE ROAD

DOCK

St. ANDREWS

River...

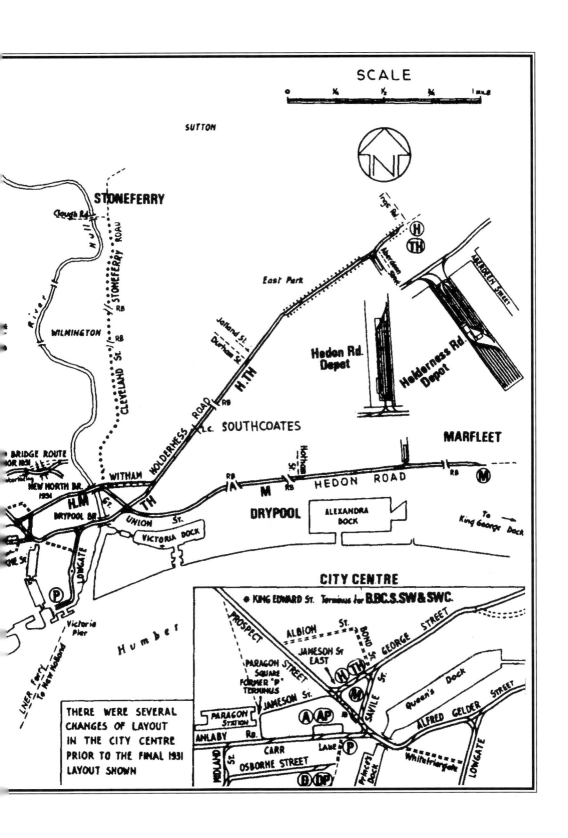

SCALE

SUTTON

STONEFERRY

East Park

Hedon Rd.
Depot

Holderness Rd.
Depot

WILMINGTON

SOUTHCOATES

MARFLEET

BRIDGE ROUTE
FOR 1931

NEW NORTH BR.
1931

WITHAM

HEDON ROAD

DRYPOOL BR.

DRYPOOL

ALEXANDRA
DOCK

To
King George Dock

UNION

VICTORIA DOCK

Victoria
Pier

Humber

LNER Ferry
To New Holland

CITY CENTRE

KING EDWARD St. Terminus for B.B.C.S.SW & SWC.

ALBION St.

GEORGE STREET

PROSPECT STREET

JAMESON St
EAST

PARAGON
SQUARE
FORMER "P"
TERMINUS

Queen's Dock

JAMESON St.

ALFRED GELDER STREET

PARAGON
STATION

ANLABY Rd.

CARR LANE

OSBORNE STREET

Princes Dock

Whitefriargate

LOWGATE

THERE WERE SEVERAL
CHANGES OF LAYOUT
IN THE CITY CENTRE
PRIOR TO THE FINAL 1931
LAYOUT SHOWN

HISTORICAL BACKGROUND

In 1871 the citizens of Kingston upon Hull enjoyed several horse drawn omnibus services. However, in that year, the Hull Tramways Act authorised the Continental and General Tramways Company to construct seven route miles comprising six horse tram routes along Holderness Road (Crown Inn), Old Town (Pier), Spring Bank, Hessle Road, Anlaby Road and Beverley Road.

These were opened between 1875 and 1877 by which time the Hull Street Tramways Company had purchased the system. In 1882 the Company carried 31,500 passengers each week using 25 trams and 121 horses. The first trailers were single deckers but thereafter double deckers were purchased of three sizes. However, the trams suffered from continued competition from horse drawn waggonnettes (called "Town Way Ups" by many local residents).

The original proposals had included Hedon Road but this was omitted from the Act. Powers to construct a tramway from North Bridge along Hedon Road to Marfleet were obtained by the Drypool and Marfleet Steam Tramways Company. Not until 22nd May 1889, did it open the route as far as Lee Smith Street, well short of Marfleet. Steam tram engines were built by Thomas Green and Son whilst the carriages were built by G F Milnes. A short branch to Drypool Bridge was added later.

There was no physical connection to enable it to reach the city centre. Negotiations for a connection with the horse system continued for many years until agreement was reached for the DMST to acquire the Holderness Road section. Yet this did not take place for reasons that remain unclear.

In the long term, neither system prospered and in 1889 the HST went into liquidation. Several attempts were made to sell the system but not until 1896 did Hull Corporation actually buy it at a cost of £12,500. A Mr W Nettleton was appointed to run the horse trams until a decision was taken about the system's future. In October 1899 the Corporation also acquired the DMST for £15,500 and ran the steam trams until 13 January 1901.

Powers were obtained in 1898 by Hull Corporation to operate electric trams. Matters proceeded quickly. On 5 July 1899, with great ceremony, the first routes to Anlaby Road and Hessle Road were opened. The opening was preceded by an acrimonious exchange of correspondence with the Board of Trade as the Corporation was anxious to start operations in time for the Great Yorkshire Agricultural Show located just beyond the Anlaby Road terminus at Newington.

Both routes were double track throughout, a feature that was repeated with every subsequent route and extension whether in the street or on a central reservation.

Two new depots were opened, at Liverpool Street (which also included the central workshops) for the Hessle Road route and at Wheeler Street on Anlaby Road. Additionally, a new electricity generating station was opened in Osborne Street in the city centre.

Further routes were opened in 1900 to Holderness Road (10th April) and Spring Bank (2nd June), which was extended to Queens Road (8th October). Beverley Road trams commenced running on 8th December. In 1902 route letters were introduced as replacements for colour lights. As far as possible the letters used were the first letter of the destination. Subsequently two, three and (for a short time) even four letters were used. Small destination screens were fitted at both ends and on each side, not always in the same position.

Within a few years of the inauguration of the system the city centre was radically altered. A new City Hall was built alongside the new central square named after Queen Victoria and slums were swept away to permit the construction of new shopping streets (King Edward Street and Jameson Street).The northern routes originally ran from Savile Street along Bond Street and Albion Street to Prospect Street. However, when King Edward Street was constructed between the newly opened Queen Victoria Square and Prospect Street and the northern routes were re-routed.

Tram 101 which arrived in 1900 was note-worthy in being the only bogie tram owned by the Corporation. It was not a success and was sold to Erith Urban District Council in 1916 where it survived until 1933.

In 1902 the fleet comprised 101 cars of which 71 were in service on weekdays and 41 on Sundays. A three-minute headway operated all day on each route with an early morning frequency for workmen of ten minutes. The fare for any distance was 1d.

The Queens Road route was extended along Newland Avenue to Cottingham Road on 19th January 1903 and the Holderness Road route was extended to Aberdeen Street on 27th March 1903. The Pier service opened on 20th October 1903 via a revised route along the recently opened Alfred Gelder Street and Lowgate. Hedon Road was electrified on 17th December 1903. Two more depots were opened: one near Aberdeen Street on Holderness Road and the other on Hedon Road.

In September 1903, car 61 was fitted with a

moveable top cover. Thirty such conversions were undertaken by 1905 when the programme was terminated as conductors were spending more time adjusting the covers than in collecting fares!

By the end of 1906 there were 116 tramcars were in stock. All were originally open top and came from a variety of manufacturers including Milnes, Brush, ER&TCW, Hurst Nelson and five from the American Brill company (cars 26-30) which were used on the Pier service.

Cars 66-90 had been delivered in 1899 as trailers numbered 101-125. They were not successful and the bodies were mounted on Brill 21E trucks before re-entering service in 1900.

An alternative route for the Holderness Road trams was introduced in July 1907, after Drypool Bridge was opened. Tracks were constructed between Lowgate (on the Pier route) and the Holderness Road/Witham junction. A triangular junction was installed at the junction of Alfred Gelder Street and Lowgate but the eastern curves saw little use.

In 1907 the Undertaking's Statutory Rules and Orders permitted a highest speed of 14 mph on Hedon Road between the carsheds and the Hull and Barnsley Railway bridge. The lowest speed restriction was a mere 2 mph when turning from Midland Street into Anlaby Road and vice versa. In several places, including level crossings, trams had "to be brought to a standstill to avoid impending danger before proceeding".

A new depot for the northern routes was opened on Cottingham Road halfway between Newland Avenue and Beverley Road in March 1909. This replaced the Stepney Lane depot which continued in use as a permanent way yard. Also in 1909 a five track tramway "station" opened in Queen Victoria Square

Six trams (117-122) were delivered from UEC in 1909. These were followed by fourteen cars (123-136) which were constructed in the department's own Liverpool Street Workshops. All possessed open balconies.

Some track was laid in Cleveland Street and across Stoneferry Bridge (on Clough Road) as part of a proposed route to Stoneferry but problems with landowners along the route caused delays and the powers lapsed, despite much local pressure.

A further twenty-four cars (137-160) were received from Brush in 1912. They also had open balconies.

On 29th April 1912 the Hedon Road route was extended to Marfleet, thirty years after the first horse tram proposals. An extension from Botanic Gardens to the Walton Street crossing along Spring Bank West was opened in time for Hull Fair week in October 1913. The next extension was opened in 1914 when the Hessle Road route was extended to Pickering Park Gates. The section between North Road and the new terminus was laid on reserved track in the central reservation.

The first fares revisions since the opening of the electric tramways were introduced on 18th May 1914. The flat fare system which had been retained despite the extensions to the system was replaced with a fare stage system.

The final batch of trams was delivered from Brush in 1915. These had open balconies but had closed lower deck vestibules. They were numbered 161 – 180.

Service cuts were instituted as a result of the war but rider ship rose by over twenty per cent. On 7th June 1915 service P was disrupted due to damage caused by an overnight attack by German airships. As many employees joined the forces conductresses were employed for the duration, despite opposition from existing staff.

In October 1914 two cars were converted into recruiting cars. Maintenance work on the infrastructure was cut back to save money and labour.

In 1919 an extension along Cottingham Road to Newland Park (a very up market housing area) and the Training College and a new service (BC) via Beverley Road was introduced. All-night services were introduced for a time in July 1919 but were withdrawn in April 1921. From November 1919 until 1923 the Newland Avenue and the Beverley Road routes were linked as a circular service. In December 1919 the Pickering Road route was linked with the Marfleet route as a cross-city facility but this innovation lasted a mere nine days!

The tramway station in Queen Victoria Square was removed in the early 1920s and the Anlaby Road and Hessle Road routes transferred to a one-way terminal loop around Waterworks Street and Chariot Street. The Hessle Road terminus was then transferred to Osborne Street in 1923, about a hundred yards from the Square.

One new tram was delivered in 1923. Numbered 101, it was constructed by EEC to the Tramways Manager's own design. This was a truckless vehicle powered by two 42 hp Dick Kerr trolleybus motors. Power was transmitted through longitudinal carden shafts with universal joints to differentials on split axles. It was totally enclosed with a seating capacity of sixty-six and was demonstrated at the Tramways Managers' Conference held in Hull during September 1923. A unique feature was the provision of a seat for the motorman!

Despite the introduction of motor bus

routes, more tramway extensions were opened. Extensions from Aberdeen Street to Ings Road (on reserved track), from Spring Bank West to Park Avenue, from Pickering Park to Pickering Road (on reserved track) and from Newington along Anlaby Road (also on reserved track) to Pickering Road, were introduced in 1925.

Hull's final tramcar entered service in 1925. Car 113 was constructed at Liverpool Street Workshops and fully enclosed with sixty-six seats.

In July 1926 the Beverley Road route was extended (mostly on reservation) to Endike Lane. Finally, the Newland Park route (BC) was extended along Cottingham Road to the junction with Hall Road. For a short time the Newland Avenue service was also extended to Hall Road (SC) but this was soon discontinued. In the financial year 1927/8 the trams carried 67,521,190 passengers.

At the start of 1930 the following tram services were believed to be in operation:

West Hull

A	Waterworks Street - Carr Lane - Anlaby Road (Boothferry Road)
AP	Waterworks Street - Carr Lane - Anlaby Road - Pickering Road North
---	Waterworks Street - Carr Lane - Anlaby Road - Walton Street (peaks and Hull Fair Week)
---	Waterworks Street – Carr lane – Anlaby Road – Boulevard (football, rugby and cricket matches)
D	Osborne Street - Porter Street - Hessle Road – Dairycoates
DP	Osborne Street – Porter Street – Hessle Road – Pickering Road South
---	Osborne Street – Porter Street – Hessle Road – West Dock Avenue (peak periods)
---	Osborne Street – Porter Street – Hessle Road – Pickering Park Gates (occasional)

North Hull

B	King Edward Street – Beverley Road – Endike Lane
BC	King Edward Street – Beverley Road – Cottingham Road (Hall Road)
QB	King Edward Street – Beverley Road – Queens Road
S	King Edward Street – Spring Bank – Princes Avenue – Newland Avenue (Cottingham Road)
SC	King Edward Street – Spring Bank – Princes Avenue – Newland Avenue – Cottingham Road (Hall Road) (peak periods)
QS	King Edward Street – Spring Bank – Princes Avenue (Queens Road) (peak periods)
SW	King Edward Street - Spring Bank – Spring Bank West – Chanterlands Avenue (Park Avenue)
SWC	King Edward Street – Spring Bank – Spring Bank West – Chanterlands Avenue North (Cottingham Road)
---	King Edward Street – Spring Bank – Spring Bank West (Walton Street) (Peak periods and Hull Fair Week)
---	Newland Avenue – Princes Avenue – Spring Bank West (Walton Street) (Hull Fair Week)

East Hull

H	Jameson Street – George Street – North Bridge – Witham – Holderness Road – Ings Road
TH	Jameson Street – Alfred Gelder Street – Drypool Bridge – Holderness Road – Ings Road
---	Jameson Street – George Street – North Bridge – Witham – Holderness Road (Durham Street) (peak periods)
M	Savile Street – George Street – Great Union Street – Hedon Road – Marfleet
P	Queen Victoria Square – Monument Bridge – Alfred Gelder Street – Lowgate – Market Place – Pier

This list is not exhaustive as there were several variations both before and after 1931.

Hull was unusual in that its rail was centre grooved with tramcar wheels being centre-flanged, possibly because the City Engineer was responsible for the design and maintenance of the track. The overhead was placed at one side of the road in several locations rather than being centrally positioned. This reduced service speeds especially where curves were tight. Side running had been the subject of much discussion with the Board of Trade before it was permitted.

The manager, Mr E S Rayner, wanted to replace the Preston Road motorbus route with trolleybuses as a possible first step towards tram replacement but, in 1930, a Town Meeting rejected this. In 1931, after many difficulties with committee members, he left and was succeeded by Mr D P Morrison from Dundee.

Soon after his arrival, the Pier route (having been reduced to a single car service) closed on 5th September 1931. In June 1932 the Holderness Road (TH) route was withdrawn when the Monument Bridge was removed as part of the filling in of Queen's Dock Mr Morrison wanted to replace side running with centre overhead in order to increase speeds but was unable to obtain the Tramways Committee's approval. His initial thoughts of replacing all the northern tram routes did not materialise.

Some modernisation continued to be undertaken. Between 1932 and 1935 eighty-two trucks of a modern design were bought second-hand. Of these, fifty-four were equipped with magnetic track brakes which were new to Hull.

In July 1934 a coordination agreement with the East Yorkshire Motor Services Company was introduced. This divided the city into an "A" area, in which the Corporation retained all revenue, equating roughly (but not entirely) with the limits of the original tram routes and a "B" area covering the rest of the city in which revenue and mileage was shared between them. A third area, "C", lay outside the city boundary and was the exclusive preserve of East Yorkshire. Different tickets were used for each area. Tram use had declined from 57.9 million in 1930/1 to 38.3 million in 1934/5.

The reserved track routes AP and DP were withdrawn, although trams remained on services A and D, along with services BC, SWC and SW, all being replaced by KHCT buses. Cottingham Road depot was closed to trams with other depots supplying the northern routes' needs.

Trams may have continued to run to Walton Street during Hull Fair Week. When Major G R S Wilson undertook the formal inspection of the Chanterlands Avenue trolleybus route in July 1937 he was informed that trams would operate to Walton Street during the fair week in October. After careful consideration, he consented to this but, in the event, trams were not used.

After the 1934 conversions the fleet was reduced to 120 tramcars with a further reduction to 115 shortly thereafter. Service speeds remained slow with passengers preferring faster and more comfortable buses.

The results of an inquiry (the third major inquiry during the tram era) into the department's performance in 1934/35 were not good. Before publication Mr Morrison left for Bournemouth and his assistant, Mr J Lawson, took over, initially on a temporary basis. He also tried, again without success, to introduce centre running and eventually recommended trolleybuses citing the high cost of renewing and improving tram tracks together with the inability to speed up tram operations.

The conversion programme started in July 1937 beginning with the abandoned Chanterlands Avenue route. The Newland Avenue route closed in October followed by Hedon Road (using buses) and Beverley Road in 1938. After a short postponement due to the outbreak of World War II, the Holderness Road route succumbed in February 1940. Not until September 1942 was the Anlaby Road route replaced. The Dairycoates route lingered until 30th June 1945 when a suitably illuminated no. 169, carrying a civic party, performed the final journey from Osborne Street.

Between 1942 and 1945 some forty-two trams were sold to Leeds where they acquired the nickname "Kipperboxes". They were withdrawn between 1945 and 1951.

Two trams lasted long enough to be preserved, car 96 at Heaton Park in Manchester and car 132 which now rests in the City's StreetLife Museum. A model of Mr Rayner's tramcar 101 which was constructed by apprentices at Liverpool Street Workshops for display in the city's pavilion at the British Empire Exhibition at Wembley in 1924 can also be found in the museum.

Today, the only reminders of the trams are some track at the entrance to the former Wheeler Street depot and a single traction pole near Hall Road.

ANLABY ROAD

1.   There were three basic designs of double deck horse cars. Car 30 which is seen here was a medium sized car dating from 1882 and seating 36. Cars were painted in a red and white livery. The location is the Boulevard level crossing in 1895.

2.   On 5th July 1899 the citizens of Kingston upon Hull turned out in large numbers to admire the new cars and to watch the opening ceremony. Trams 4 and 26 are shown in St John Street before setting off on the first journeys. Behind them is the Wilberforce Monument which stood there until its relocation in 1936.

3.   Another view of car 26 on the opening day illustrates the layout of the upper deck and the diverse range of hats on view. Car 26 was one of five trams built by Brill in Pittsburg which had upholstered seating (unlike its contemporaries) and curtains.

4.   Car 60, which had the dubious honour of being the first electric tram to be withdrawn around 1919, passes the Paragon Railway Station forecourt and its ornate gates. Semaphores were placed in Midland Street and in Anlaby Road. The cabin was operated by Tramways Department staff and lasted until 1923, at least, when services D and DP were diverted to Osborne Street. The track remained in use until 1942 to enable trams to reach the main workshops in Liverpool Street.

5.   Car 11 in original condition is caught by the camera on a deserted Anlaby Road, the exact location being unknown.

6.   Tram 31 passes the end of Walton Street down which the annual Hull Fair takes place. Additional tram journeys which supplemented the three minute headway during the fair week used the crossover at this point to return to the city centre.

7.   The tram approaching the camera is car 18 one of the original trams which inaugurated the route in 1899. This has received a top cover.

8.   After the abandonment of the section from Boothferry Road to Pickering Road the truncated Anlaby Road service terminus was located in a short spur along Boothferry Road. Trams 20 and 163 are shown at this location on 7 July 1937. Note the different styles of livery application, route letter and destination blinds.

9.   Five years later, in 1942, shortly before the route was abandoned, car 142 arrives at the terminus from the city centre.

HESSLE ROAD

10.   Tram 106 makes steady progress along Hessle Road possibly near West Dock Avenue, where a crossover was provided near here for peak workings.

11.   This unidentified car is passing the junction with Boulevard. On the corner of South Boulevard is St Barnabas church, and the memorial erected in memory of fisherman killed in 1906 by the Russian fleet, which mistook the Hull trawlers for Japanese warships!

12.   In June 1938 car 106 is travelling along Porter Street away from the city centre. Its trolley boom is almost at right angles to the overhead; this style of overhead could lend itself to dewirements.

13.　　Two open top balcony trams, 145 and 146, stand at the Pickering Road terminus of route DP. In the 1930s, the open balcony cars were concentrated on the western routes.

14.   Another photograph of car 106, which shows how much it had been modernised. It is seen approaching the Dairycoates terminus.

15.   This photograph shows car 140 at the Dairycoates terminus towards the end of World War II. It also illustrates the track layout which had permitted trams working to Pickering Road (DP) to avoid the trams standing at the D terminus and then continue unhindered.

SPRING BANK

16.   Spring Bank was originally a pleasant thoroughfare lined with trees down the centre of the road. These are shown to good effect in this shot of cars 35 and 61. As road traffic increased, the trees were removed. Level crossings were protected by catch points and a semaphore signal placed on a traction pole either side of the crossing, except at Boulevard. These were controlled by the railway signalman in the adjacent box. The Corporation paid part of the signalman's wages in accordance with an agreement with the NER and (later) LNER. When the Spring Bank route was extended in 1901, the necessary equipment was not yet in place, so passengers had to alight on one side of the crossing in order to board another tram on the other side for a short period. A similar situation occurred at Dairycoates in 1914. The semaphore which guarded the level crossing can be seen on the traction pole on the right. When "off" in the down position, the signal permitted trams to proceed. When "on" in the horizontal position, the gates were closed to road traffic.

17.   This view of car 37 looks towards the level crossing and the gardens beyond. Although called Botanic Gardens locals simply referred to the location as "Botanic".

18.   Trams working as far as the junction of Queens Road with Princes Avenue were designated QS. Car 47 is seen leaving Spring Bank at Blundell's Corner and is about to enter Prospect Street. The buildings on the left would shortly be demolished to make way for the new Ferensway road.

19.   Tram 124 swings into Spring Bank from Princes Avenue en route to the city centre, the destination box notwithstanding. Throughout the tramway era heavy delays were experienced at level crossings. In 1924 a survey revealed that that the Anlaby Road (Boulevard) crossing was negotiated by 310 scheduled tram journeys a day from 0530 to 2336. Throughout the city, gates were closed to road traffic for one quarter of the day! Nearly half of those trams affected were delayed for more than three minutes.

PRINCES AVENUE

20.   This 1904 view of 70 at the southern end of Princes Avenue shows how the tram track swung to the right before turning left over the level crossing into Spring Bank.

21.   This is a much later view at the same location with tram 116 waiting for the gates to open. The semaphore that guarded this section can be clearly seen on the traction pole on the right.

22.   On what is probably a Saturday (given the wedding car) tram 124 awaits authorisation from the point duty policeman at the Botanic Gardens crossing. Of interest are the track and overhead leading from Princes Avenue into Spring Bank West, which were normally only used during the Hull Fair Week in October.

23.   Car 110 makes its way through the leafy northern half of Princes Avenue near the "Avenues" area outward bound for Newland Avenue.

24.   Two fountains were to be found in the "Avenues" area of Princes Avenue. This one was located outside the entrance to Pearson Park. Car 30 is negotiating the fountain on its way to the city centre. When the fountains were removed to ease the traffic flow, the rails were not "straightened"!

25.   Car 88 pauses to unload passengers near Queens Road. This tram was originally placed in service as trailer car 123 in 1899, but these trailers were not a success. Therefore, all were "electrified" in 1900. This location is much the same today.

26.   Tram 148 progresses majestically along an almost deserted Queens Road on its way to Newland Avenue.

NEWLAND AVENUE

27.   Although car 33 carries a "B" route letter, it is standing outside the Monica cinema on Newland Avenue. The photograph is not dated, so one can only speculate whether this was taken during 1919-1923, when the Beverley Road and Newland Avenue services were operated as a circular service.

28.   All of the tram routes enjoyed an intensive service and it was not unusual to see several trams at some outer termini.Cars 85 and 149, together with a third, congregate at the Newland Avenue terminus. The curve in the foreground leads into the western part of Cottingham Road and was used for a short time in the late twenties by service SC to Hall Road.

29. Despite showing Spring Bank in the destination box, car 122 is standing at the Newland Avenue terminus of route S. In the background are the Sailors' Orphans Homes, which held a gala on every Whit Monday.

COTTINGHAM ROAD

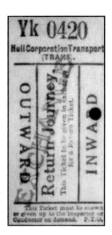

30. This unidentified tram is pictured outside Cottingham Road Depot. Note that the depot offices are of single storey construction. During the late 1920s a second storey was added, and the complete building still survives as offices.

———————▶

31.　　The extensions along Cottingham Road from Newland Avenue were opened in two sections. The first, to Newland Park (a very prestigious residential area) which also adjoined the Training College, was opened in 1919. Tram 58 is shown on route BC near Newland Park.

32.　　The second extension opened in July 1926. This continued along Cottingham Road past Chanterlands Avenue to the Goodfellowship Inn near Hall Road. It served private housing near the terminus and council housing on the northern side of Cottingham Road. Car 113, which was the last tram to be placed in service, is pictured near the terminus. The shops in the background were new and still exist today.

———————▶

33.　　This view of the interior of the upper deck of a tram was taken at Hall Road. Note the route letters and the wooden seating and the layout of the seats. Headroom looks a little cramped.

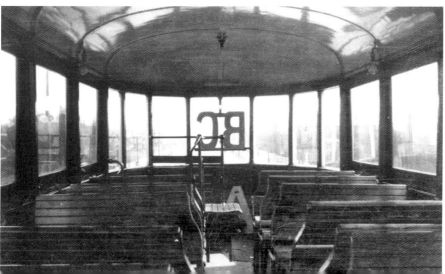

34.   After 27th July 1934, the service along Cottingham Road to Hall Road was withdrawn as part of the coordination agreement with East Yorkshire Motor Services. Trams on the Beverley Road route which terminated at Cottingham Road were given the "BN" designation as carried by cars 116 and 148.

WEEKDAYS.

Route Letter.	Route.	City Terminus	Outer Terminus	To City. First Car	To City. Last Car	From City. First Car	From City. Last Car	Ordinary Service Minutes
D	Hessle Road	Osborne Street	Dairycoates	6-30 a.m.	10-48 p.m.	6-45 a.m.	11-0 p.m.	3
A	Anlaby Road	Waterworks St.	Wheeler St.	*5-0 a.m.	10-45 p.m.	5-15 a.m.	11-0 p.m.	3
H	Holderness Rd.	Jameson St.	Ings Road	4-55 a.m.	10-42 p.m.	5-18 a.m.	11-0 p.m.	3

EARLY MORNING CARS.

*Anlaby Road.—To City : 5-0 a.m., 5-15 a.m., 5-30 a.m., 5-45 a.m., 6-0 a.m.
   From City : 5-15 a.m., 5-30 a.m., 5-45 a.m., 6-0 a.m., 6-15 a.m., 6-30 a.m.
Holderness Road—To City : 4-55 a.m., 5-12 a.m. and every 12 minutes till 6-24 a.m.
   From City : 5-18 a.m., 5-30 a.m., 5-45 a.m., 5-54 a.m., 6-6 a.m., 6-18 a.m.

SUNDAYS.

Route Letter.	Route	City Terminus	Outer Terminus	To City First Car	To City Last Car	From City First Car	From City Last Car	Ordinary Service Minutes
D	Hessle Road	Osborne St.	Dairycoates	9-3 a.m.	12-51 p.m.	9-15 a.m.	12-51 p.m.	12
				1-0 p.m.	10-6 p.m.	1-14 p.m.	10-20 p.m.	3
A	Anlaby Road	Waterworks St.	Wheeler St.	1-0 p.m.	10-4 p.m.	1-16 p.m.	10-20 p.m.	4
H	Holderness Rd.	Jameson St.	Ings Road	1-0 p.m.	10-4 p.m.	1-17 p.m.	10-20 p.m.	4

Night Service Fares are charged on all cars running after the following times :—

   To City, 10-10 p.m.   From City, 10-27 p.m.

Sunday Morning Service Fares are charged on all cars running before the following times :—

   To City, 1-0 p.m.   From City, 1-0 p.m.

BEVERLEY ROAD

35.   Horse tram 11, which is returning to the city centre, has just crossed the Stepney station level crossing on Beverley Road. The station and yard entrance can be seen behind the tram. This type of trailer was one of the large trailers which were delivered in 1870 and seated 44.

36.   Another large horse tram car 15, is caught by the camera near the loop at Lambert Street sometime in 1895.

37. Car 92 has just passed under the Hull and Barnsley Railway Bridge on its way to the city centre. A street to the left of the tram led to the HBR station in Fitzroy Street.

38. When it snows this much today, everything stops, but the trams just kept going. Two unidentified snow-covered cars are seen on Beverley Road

39. This location is the original Beverley Road terminus near Cottingham Road and the photograph shows the original "Haworth Arms" public house. This was demolished when Beverley Road was extended northwards and a replacement was built on the corner of the new road and Cottingham Road.

40. A sylvan scene near the Beverley Road Baths through which car 80 is travelling to the city centre. Note how the trees have grown since photograph 37 was taken.

41.   Car 115 is about to turn left into Cottingham Road on its way to Hall Road. The new Haworth (pronounced locally as "Hayworth") Arms public house (see photograph 39) can be clearly seen.

42.   In June 1938, car 132 prepares to cross the junction with Cottingham Road on its way to Endike Lane. On the left the trolleybus overhead is in place and almost ready for the conversion in September. This tram was sold to Leeds, but is now preserved in the City's Streetlife Museum.

43.   In July 1926 the Beverley Road route was extended and the section from Inglemire Lane to Endike Lane was laid on a central reservation. car 148 is shown at the new terminus.

44.　　Car 71 enters Prospect Street from Beverley Road en route for King Edward Street. The lines from the right come from Spring Bank. All the buildings in this view have since been demolished.

TRAMWAY FARE STAGES.

Route Letter	Route	1d. Stages.	1½d. Stages.	2d. Stages.
D	Hessle Road	Osborne Street and Neptune Street	.... Osborne Street and .... Dairycoates	—
		Neptune Street and Dairycoates	....	
A	Anlaby Road	.... Waterworks Street and Linnaeus Street	.... Waterworks Street and .... Wheeler Street	—
		Linnaeus Street and Wheeler Street	....	

HOLDERNESS ROAD

45.   On what must be an early Sunday morning, an unidentified open top tram glides along Holderness Road. As Hull extended its main roads, tree planting on a generous scale was carried out. Today much pruning has been undertaken to meet the demands of modern traffic.

46.   A pristine looking car 160 rests at the Holderness Road terminus which was located a few yards short of the junction with Ings Road and Maybury Road.

47.   Also at this terminus on 7th July 1937 is car 140, which has just arrived from "town". The trolley reverser can be clearly seen. These were provided at all outer termini, apart from DP at Pickering Road and BN at Newland. The quiet nature of this eastern suburb is unbelievable with only a single motor car in view.

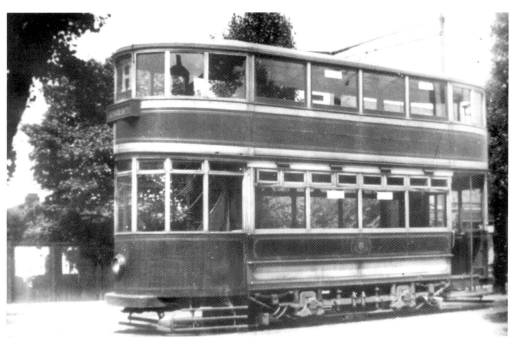

49.   In 1939 car 118 is pictured near the terminus. As can be seen, not all Hull's trams possessed fully domed roofs, the profile on this car being relatively flat.

48.   Car 140 is seen near Southcoates Avenue en route for the city centre.

HEDON ROAD

50.	The steam engines (this is no. 4) were built by Greens of Leeds and the trailers by G F Milnes of Birkenhead. The lack of advertisements suggests that this photograph was taken when they were fairly newly in service.

 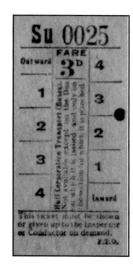

51.   Everyone in view watches the cameraman and ignores engine (believed to be no. 7) and trailer. This photograph is thought to date from around 1896. In contrast with the previous photograph, the engine and trailer are now festooned with advertisements.

52.   The Hull and Barnsley Railway Bridge that crossed Hedon Road was one of seven that crossed tram routes as the line wended its roundabout way to the eastern docks. Tram 80 is taking on passengers near the Alexandra Dock Gates.

53.   The route letters MA, as carried by car 54, originally denoted workings that had been extended to Marfleet Avenue.

54.   Tram 89, looking a little careworn, is seen on Hedon Road on 27th March 1937. Hedon Road was not as financially sound as other routes since housing was concentrated on the northern side of the road, the other side having the docks and associated marine engineering companies.

PIER

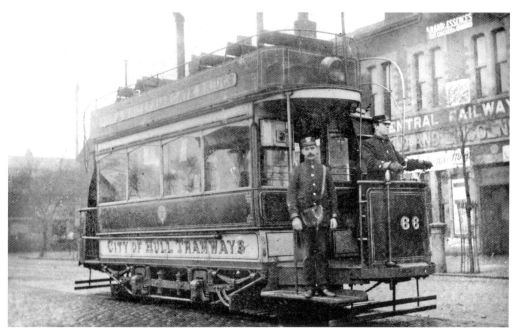

55.   The Victoria or Corporation Pier was located in the Old Town on the River Humber. The ferries that sailed between here and New Holland in Lincolnshire were operated by the Great Central Railway (later LNER and BR), whose offices can be seen in the background. Tram 66 (previously trailer 102) awaits passengers before returning to Queen Victoria Square.

TRAMWAY FARE STAGES

Route Letter	Route	1d. Stages	1½d. Stages	2d. Stages
H	Holderness Road	Jameson Street and Dansom Lane	Jameson Street and Durham Street	Jameson Street and Ings Road
		Dansom Lane and Durham Street	Dansom Lane and Ings Road	—
		Durham Street and Ings Road	—	—

CHILDREN'S FARES—
        Children at 3 and under 14 years   ....   ½d.

SCHOLARS' FARES—
        Scholars 14 to 16 years, when travelling to and from School .... 1d. (Prepaid Ticket) for any distance.

WORKMEN'S FARES up to and including 9 a.m.
        Between —City and Outer Terminus on any one Route .... 1d. single.
        (Up to and including 8 a.m. .... 1d. single, 2d. return).

SPECIAL 1d. TRANSFER TICKET, available for use on Service 62 Trolley Bus) and Service 21 Omnibus between Cottingham Grove and Queen's Road (S.).

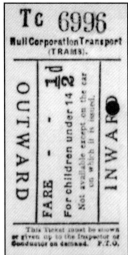

Tc 6996

Hull Corporation Transport
(TRAMS).

OUTWARD

FARE 1/2

For children under 14

Not available except on the car
on which it is issued.

INWARD

This Ticket must be shown
or given up to the Inspector of
Conductor on demand. P.T.O.

56. Tram 28 had received an enclosed upper saloon (but not enclosed balconies). It waits patiently for passengers before setting out for the city centre.

57. An unidentified tram prepares to turn left from Lowgate into Alfred Gelder Street on its journey back to Monument Bridge. On the left is St Mary's Church with the General Post office on the right. Both buildings remain in situ but the latter is now converted into several flats.

58.   During the horse tram era Whitefriargate was an important shopping street. This photograph from 1892 seems to confirm that status. The single track is located rather awkwardly alongside the northern side of the street. When the system was electrified, the trams to the Pier were routed along the newly built Alfred Gelder Street to Lowgate.

59.   Savile Street was another important shopping street. It was traversed by the northern horse tram routes including the Beverley Road route whose cars worked across the Old Town to the Victoria. Pier The destination board on car 1 (which dates from 1879) is a little lopsided! Also to be seen are several waggonnettes drawn up at the kerbside. It is thought that this view is from 1892.

60.   When the electric services to Beverley Road and Spring Bank were opened, the trams followed the same route as the horse trams along Prospect Street, Albion Street and Bond Street to Savile Street. When the new King Edward Street was opened, they were re-routed along the lower part of Prospect and the new street to Queen Victoria Square. Here an unidentified tram is turning from Prospect Street into Albion Street. The tram seems dwarfed by the buildings around it.

61. Tram 91 is seen at work on route TH, which ran from the city centre via Drypool Bridge and Holderness Road. Note that the destination blind says "Ings Lane" not "Ings Road".

62. In 1913 Tram 142 in has just left King Edward Street and has entered Prospect Street. Compare the condition of 142 with the same tram in Osborne Street in its final form in photograph 76.

63.	Tram 136 is shown in Prospect Street in company with Guy FCX no. 49 on the Preston Road route. This bus was originally ordered as a trolleybus for that route but electors vetoed the proposal. Although twenty years older than the bus it can be argued that the tram looks the more modern of the two.

65.	Tram 108 is nearest the camera in King Edward Street. Note the comparison between the fully enclosed trams and the one behind, which still retains open balcony and open vestibules.

64.	An early view of King Edward Street shows tram 95 having centre stage.

Io 2009

Hull Corporation Transport
(TRAMS)

Outward

This Ticket must be shown or given up to the Inspector or Conductor on demand.	P.T.O.

Vr 7936

Hull Corporation Transport
(TRAMS).

Outward

This Ticket must be shown or given up to the Inspector or Conductor on demand.	P.T.O.

66. Car 130 awaits departure time in King Edward Street. Its "BC" route will take it to Hall Road via Beverley Road and Cottingham Road. Note the method of showing destination and via information.

67. Trolley reversers were not provided in the city centre, so conductors, such as the one shown here in charge of car 172, had to change the direction of the trolley boom, even though they had to stand in the middle of the road to do so! The destination is shown as Anlaby Road, but the terminus for that route was in Waterworks Street (behind the photographer).

68.   Trams 11 and 22 leave the city centre via Carr Lane. This scene has changed completely. All the buildings on the right have now been replaced with modern blocks. The Wilberforce Monument now lies in Wilberforce Drive.

69.   This is St John Street in 1899 with tram 11 and a trailer car. The latter is distinguished by its red decency panels. The trailers were converted to electric cars in 1900.

70.   Two trams on the Dairycoates and Anlaby Road routes enter Queen Victoria Square from Carr Lane. Behind them is the imposing frontage of the City Hall.

71.   Trams from four routes can be seen around the "tramway station" in Queen Victoria Square. This seems to be a comparatively quiet scene, given that six routes used this section and that twenty journeys an hour on each route were timetabled at peak times.

72. On 15th March 1931, car 142 stands in Queen Victoria Square before departing for the Pier. Behind are the Dock Offices (Docks headquarters), which adjoin the Queens Dock.

73. Two trams (the nearest being car 16 from 1899) cross Monument Bridge. Queens Dock is on the right and Princes Dock is on the left.

74. Car 71 is shown on Monument Bridge on 15th March 1931, six months before the route closed. This photograph shows clearly the overhead arrangement at this point.

75. In 1920 the Anlaby Road and Hessle Road termini were transferred to Waterworks Street (renamed Paragon Street in 1952). Car 136 stands surrounded by buildings that were mostly destroyed in World War II.

76. After only three years in Waterworks Street, the Hessle Road terminus was moved once more, this time to Osborne Street, partly in response to the entreaties of shopkeepers, but mostly to eliminate delays caused at the Midland Street/Anlaby Road junction. Osborne Street was used by horse trams until electrification in 1899. With the large Willis's department store behind it car 142 stands at the terminus.

77. It is 1943 and car 142 is again standing at the Osborne Street terminus, this time with the bomb damaged Willis site behind it.

78.   When the electric trams were introduced, the Holderness Road route terminated in Savile Street. When the eastern extension of Jameson Street was opened, the terminus was transferred to the point where car 100 is standing. The date is around 1936.

80.   Four years later, in 1935, car 80 is outward bound for Ings Road. The bridge required special arrangements to enable the power to be maintained.

79.   On 10th August 1931, the new North Bridge was opened. Car 92 is about to cross the bridge from Witham towards the city centre. Note the policeman on point duty.

FINALE

81. To commemorate the end of the tramway system, car 169 was chosen to work the last journey of all. It was suitably decorated to mark the occasion and is shown here inside Liverpool Street Workshops.

82. Car 169 was also posed in full illuminated form at Liverpool Street.

83. It is 10.45 pm and car 169 is about to work the final journey of all from Osborne Street to Dairycoates. The Civic Party, having had an official supper at the Guildhall, are on board. Large crowds have gathered to watch the final journey.

ROLLING STOCK – ELECTRIC TRAMS

Throughout their lives most Hull trams were subject to many modifications (from as early as 1900!) and it is impossible to convey, in detail, the extent of these changes. At times in the twenties and thirties, it seems that no two trams were identical. Paul, one of the joint authors of this book, recently acquired a note book formerly belonging to the Chief Engineer, Mr A Turner. This contains many useful pieces of information about the trams and his own fleet summary uses names by which batches were known by staff. They are mentioned in this part of the text.

Trams carried a principal colour of crimson lake. Panels were edged in black and lined gold with elaborate corner decoration. Window pillars, rails and canopies were broken white as were rocker panels, although they were lined in crimson lake. An elaborate coat of arms was carried on the centre side panel below the lower saloon windows. Trucks were painted black. Roofs were in matt crimson. Until 1919 the rocker panels carried the legend CITY OF HULL TRAMWAYS in gold shaded black to right and below.

From 1933 most of the enclosed cars that were to be retained had two horizontal bands of broken white around the upper saloon panels. At first a small number received pale lilac. Roofs became white and trucks bauxite red. Panel edging was in umber with black being completely eliminated. Where possible, the coat-of-arms appeared on the ends of the upper saloons.

84.   **1-15 G F Milnes 1898**

We have included three photographs which illustrate the stages in the life of the first batch of electric trams. This is a fine side view of car 5 in as delivered condition. It shows how little protection was given to upper deck passengers, who seem to be in a precarious position. It was probably just as well that service speeds were low! Note the curtains in the lower saloon and the exposed driving position.

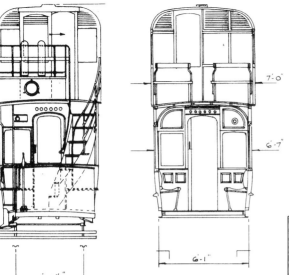

HULL CITY TRAMWAYS
DOUBLE DECK BOGIE CAR

Built: Milnes 1900.
Fleet No. 101.
See note.

Scale: 4   mm = 1Foot.

DRAWING No. TC710

SCALE
FEET   0 1 2 3 4 5 6 7 8 9 10 11 12

7'-0"

6'-7"

6'-1"

4'-8½"
TRACK GAUGE
CENTRE GROOVE RAILS

This car was built without a top cover but one was added by H.C.T. in 1909. The car was sold to Erith Corporation Tramways in 1916 and was fleet number 19. I have created this drawing before being lost forever, using detailed and dimensioned sketches of the car made in 1938 by Walter Gratwicke whilst on the scrap line in London's Brixton Hill depot.   Terry Russell May 2005.

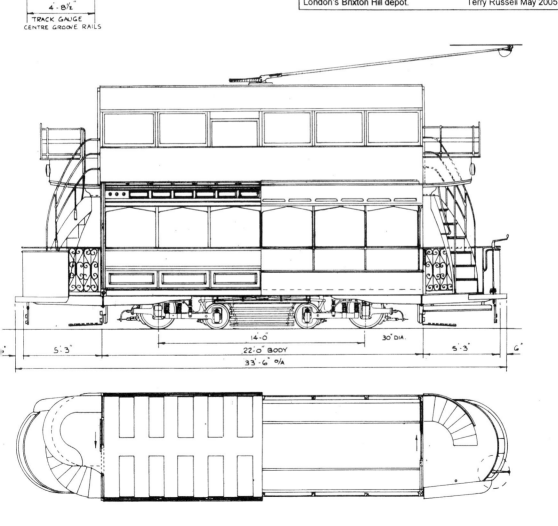

14'-0"   30" DIA.
22'-0" BODY
5'-3"   33'-6" O/A   5'-3"

DRAWN BY:-TERRY RUSSELL, "CHACESIDE", ST.LEONARDS PARK, HORSHAM, W.SUSSEX. RH13 6EG.
SEND 4 FIRST CLASS STAMPS FOR COMPLETE LIST OF PUBLIC TRANSPORT DRAWINGS.

85.   Tram 2 is shown when in an intermediate stage with a top cover, but retaining open balconies and vestibules. The curtains are no longer provided.

86.   By 1928, tram 4 had received fully enclosed balconies and vestibules. Seating capacity had been increased from 51 to 66. Compare this with the previous photograph and the reader can see how much modification and modernisation was carried out on individual trams. It can be appreciated how much extra weight had been added with a detrimental effect on the power/weight ratio.

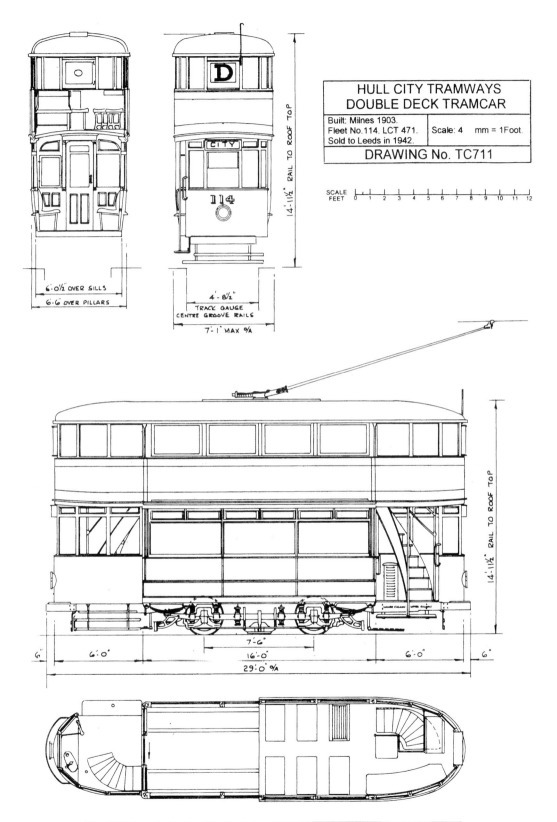

14'-11½" RAIL TO ROOF TOP

6'-0½" OVER SILLS
6'-6 OVER PILLARS

4'-8½"
TRACK GAUGE
CENTRE GROOVE RAILS

7'-1" MAX O/A

**HULL CITY TRAMWAYS
DOUBLE DECK TRAMCAR**

| Built: Milnes 1903.
Fleet No.114. LCT 471.
Sold to Leeds in 1942.	Scale: 4 mm = 1Foot.

DRAWING No. TC711

SCALE FEET   0 1 2 3 4 5 6 7 8 9 10 11 12

6"   6'-0"   7'-6"   16'-0"   6'-0"   6"

29'-0" O/A

DRAWN BY:-TERRY RUSSELL, "CHACESIDE", ST.LEONARDS PARK, HORSHAM, W.SUSSEX. RH13 6EG.
SEND 4 FIRST CLASS STAMPS FOR COMPLETE LIST OF PUBLIC TRANSPORT DRAWINGS.

→

88.   26-30 Brill 1899

This photograph of car 28 provides an idea of the intermediate stages of modernisation, with a roof fitted whilst retaining an open balcony and vestibule. They were known (predictably) as "Americans".

87.   16-25 G F Milnes 1899

Car 22 is pictured shortly after entering service and is in original condition.

→

89.   31-60 Brush 1900

Car 33 is also at the Pier and displays an intermediate stage with a top cover. Known as "Loughboroughs".

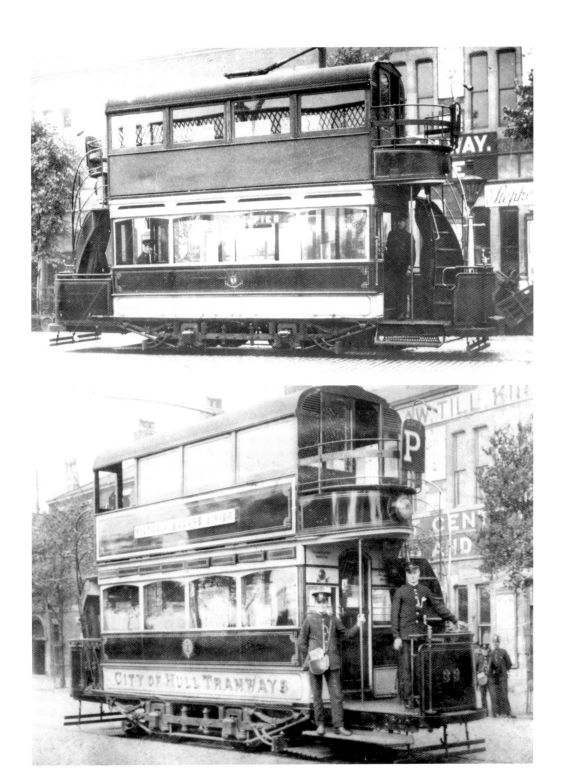

←

90. 61-65 Electric Railway and Tramway Carriage Works Ltd 1900

Tram 61 was the first to be fitted with a Kennington moveable top cover in 1903. They were not very successful, as conductors spent a great deal of time adjusting them to the detriment of fare collection! Earned the name " Old Preston Cars".

←

91. 66-90 G F Milnes 1900

Car 79 was one of twenty-five trailer cars that were delivered in 1900. They were not a success and the bodies were mounted on motorised trucks before re-entering service from 1901. Even after rebuilding they retained the title "Trailers".

92. 91-100 Hurst Nelson 1901

Another tram in original condition is car 96 (nicknamed "Motherwells") seen here in King Edward Street.

---

101 G F Milnes 1900

The one that got away! This was later sold to Erith in Kent and is illustrated in the companion Middleton Press album *North Kent Tramways*.

93.　102-116 G F Milnes 1903

By 1910, car 107 had received a top cover as shown in this photograph. The location is Ocean Place. The buildings on the left survive but are now on the corner of Ferensway which was constructed in the 1930s. "New Milnes" was their sobriquet.

──────▶

94.　117-122 Union Electric Car Company Ltd 1909

Car 119 shows the livery and lining to good effect in what looks to be a posed shot just outside Liverpool Street Depot on 7 July 1935. It had been delivered with open vestibules and open balconies, but had received enclosed vestibules around 1920. According to some records car 119 had been rebuilt and was totally enclosed by this date! Known as the "New Prestons"

──────▶

95.　123-136 Hull City Tramways 1909/10

Car 136 is seen in its final fully enclosed form with a seating capacity of 66. It is pictured at Newland Avenue. Behind the car are the Sailors Orphans Homes and the Hull Corporation Telephone Department's green and cream telephone box, a much photographed box in tram and trolleybus days. The homes and telephone box are still there today. Until 1935 there was also a timekeeper's office here. Some trolleybus overhead is already in place.

96.   137-160 Brush 1912

During the First World War several conductresses were employed to take the places of men who were in the armed forces. This is Miss Annie Winter on board tram 144 (a New Loughborough, a term which also applied to cars 161 to 180) in 1915.

97.   161-180 Brush 1915

Car 172 still retained its open balcony when photographed outside Liverpool Street Depot in 1936. This car, for some reason, did not have its balconies enclosed as did the rest of the class and it retained this layout until withdrawal.

98.   **101 English Electric 1923**

Car 101 was constructed by English Electric to the design of the then manager, Mr E S Rayner. It was fully enclosed and even included a seat for the motorman! Its unconventional truck was powered by two DK trolleybus motors and was demonstrated to MPTA delegates who were meeting in Hull. Being non-standard, it was an early casualty, lasting less than a decade in service.

99.   **113 Hull City Tramways 1925**

This was last car to be built for KHCT and was constructed at the Liverpool Street Workshops. It seated 66 passengers and was fully enclosed with full upholstered seating. It is seen here on 1st December 1944 at the Dairycoates terminus complete with motorman and conductress.

SERVICE CARS

100.   Car 96 was delivered as a standard tram in 1901. In 1933 it was converted into a works car and snow plough. It was subsequently sold to Leeds Corporation and is now preserved at Heaton Park.

101.   Car 96 was photographed, as preserved, at Heaton Park.

102.   Hull possessed two identical water carriers like this unidentified one.

PRINCES ROAD (QUEEN'S ROAD)—CHAPMAN STREET.

Service No. 28

Princes Road					
1d.	Haworth Arms				
1d.	1d.	Oak Road			
1½d.	1d.	1d.	Stoneferry Road		
1½d.	1½d.	1d.	1d.	Chamberlain Road	
2d.	1½d.	1½d.	1d.	1d.	Chapman Street

Children of 3 and under 14 years of age : Half Adult Fare (Minimum 1d.).

SUTTON CHURCH—BELLFIELD AVENUE (HOLDERNESS ROAD).

Service No. 29

Sutton Church		
1d.	Sutton Park Golf Course	
2d.	1d.	Bellfield Avenue (Holderness Road)

Children at 3 and under 14 years—Half Adult Fares.

CITY—STONEFERRY via CHARLES STREET.

Service No. 30

Coach Station					
1½d.	George Street				
1½d.	1d.	St. Paul's Church			
1½d.	1d.	1d.	Northumberland Avenue		
1½d.	1½d.	1d.	1d.	Dalton Street	
2d.	1½d.	1½d.	1d.	1d.	New Pin Offices
2d.	2d.	1½d.	1½d.	1d.	1d.	Stoneferry Green

SPECIAL OCCASIONS

103.   Trams were hired for many outings by Sunday Schools and other social institutions. On 18th August 1906 two cars have been hired by the Olive Branch Lodge of the Free Gardeners to take some two hundred school children to Newland on their annual outing.

104.   In the First World War two cars were fitted out as recruiting cars to persuade men to join
the Colours. This unidentified tram is about to leave for Holderness Road. Potential volunteers
were given a free ride to the recruiting office!

105.   Hull had a habit of decorating cars for special occasions. This car was decorated for Civic Week in October 1929 and carried nearly 1200 lamps in the city council's colours of blue and gold.

DEPOTS AND WORKSHOPS

Horse cars were kept in three permanent depots on Hessle Road (near Regent Street), Beverley Road at Temple Street and Holderness Road (near Durham Street). The steam tram depot was located at Hotham Street.

Electric Cars were housed in five depots. Trams were allocated to a particular route and were physically separated within the depot. A fleet of 180 tramcars was in stock of which 109 were in service on Sundays, 136 on weekdays and 161 on Saturdays. The Saturday turnout was 30 from Liverpool Street, 51 from Cottingham Road, 12 from Hedon Road, 39 from Anlaby Road and 29 from Holderness Road.

106. Horse tram no. 4 poses for the camera in Temple Street near the depot.

107. The final horse tram, car 23, flies a black flag to mark the occasion, prepares to enter Temple Street depot for the last time on 30th September 1899.

INSTRUCTIONS AS TO SPEED, &c.

Hessle Road Route.

1. Cars passing Walker Street and St. James Street not to exceed 6 miles per hour.

Anlaby Road Route.

2. All cars approaching the Railway Crossing in either direction must be stopped 25 yards away from the gates. When the gates are closed, they must remain there until the road is clear ; when open, they should proceed on hearing the bell. Cars must not cross the railway lines faster than 4 miles and hour.

3. Cars passing Waterhouse Lane not to exceed 4 miles and hour.

Holderness Road Route.

4. Cars should be stopped before passing Wincolmlee.

5. They should not go faster than 4 miles an hour over North Bridge and when going through facing points.

6. The above regulations apply to both inward and outward cars.

Spring Bank Route.

7. Inward cars to stop at the junction of Spring Bank and Beverley Road.

Hedon Road Route.

8. Cars in both directions to stop before passing Clarence Street.

9. Inward cars to stop before turning corner to North Bridge.

Signals at Railway Crossings.

10. All cars approaching the Railway Crossing in either direction must be stopped five yards away from the catch points, at the white mark. If the signal is against the cars, they must remain standing until the signal is dropped and the road clear. When the signal is down the car should be started on the Conductor's bell being rung, but in starting from the white mark the signal should be watched **UNTIL THE CAR HAS GONE PAST IT.**

Strict care must be taken, by both Driver and Conductor, to observe the signal, as contact with the catch points will throw the car off the line. If anything obstruct the view of the signal, or if it be absent or imperfectly shown, it must be taken to be **against.**

Speed over the railway lines must not exceed 4 miles an hour.

Any man disobeying these instructions, **FOR ANY REASON WHATEVER,** will be liable to instant dismissal.

108. Stepney Lane had only a short career as an electric tram depot. This is fine study of employees and trams and it also shows the range of uniforms that were worn by staff.

109.   When Stepney Lane closed its allocation was transferred to the new Cottingham Road depot. This interior view of Cottingham Road Depot (known locally as "Cott Road") shows how light and commodious the building was. Its capacity was seventy eight cars, but this number was never allocated here. The cars are 57, 30, 67, Water Carrier 2, 70 and 87. According to the back of the photograph, the date is 31st September 1909!

110.   This photograph focuses on cars 70 and 87 which are in the previous photograph. However, the date on this is 1918! This illustrates the perils of research and the need to treat some dates with caution. Both would seem to have been taken not long after the depot opened in 1909.

111.   Holderness Road Depot, which was opened in 1903, had a capacity of thirty cars. An adjacent extension with a further capacity of eighteen cars was subsequently constructed. The handsome façade is shown here along with tram 58 which was delivered in 1900.

112.   There were extensive sidings at the rear of the depot, as shown here. We have been unable to discover why such trackage was provided, since the depot's covered capacity was thirty-eight, well in excess of the maximum output of twenty-nine.

113. Newly-delivered cars were assembled in the recently opened Liverpool Street Workshops. The shops were kept very busy in the early days with over 100 trams being placed in service. At the rear are some of the short-lived trailer cars.

114. We have another view of cars being assembled. In later years the workshops were to construct trams.

115. This view show the workshops, and in particular the traverser that was installed in 1917.

116.   Adjoining the shops was the running shed for the Hessle Road routes. Trams 166 and 141 share space with works car 96.

117.   An interior view of Anlaby Road depot on 7 July 1937 shows trams 179, 161 and 180, all of which still possess open balconies, and the Rail Grinder.

LEEDS SERVICE

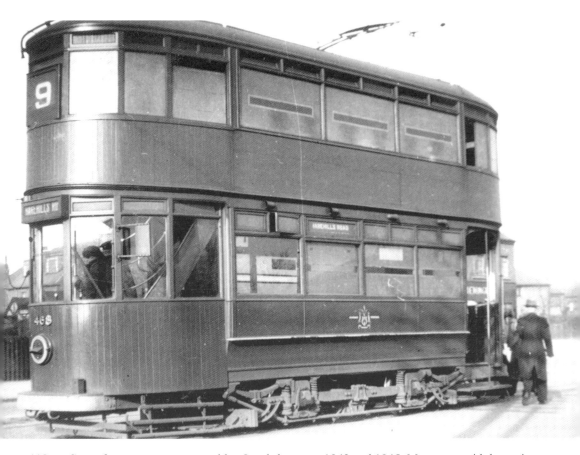

118.   Some forty-two cars were sold to Leeds between 1942 and 1945. Most were withdrawn in 1950 and 1951, as the ex-London Felthams entered service. Leeds car 468 seen here on service 9 and was formerly KHCT 174.

119. This is Leeds car 446 working on service 4. This was formerly car 132 and was stored in Leeds after withdrawal until 2 June 1955 when it was collected by the Tramway Museum Society. It had been used for an LRTL tour in 1955 of Leeds. This vehicle was the first Hull car to enter service in Leeds and was the last to be withdrawn.

PRESERVATION

120.   When car 132 arrived in Hull, it was stored in Cottingham Road Garage to enable restoration work to be carried out. This shows it leaving "Cott Road", the last tram to do so, as it began its journey to the Streetlife Museum in Hull's Old Town.

MP Middleton Press

Easebourne Lane, Midhurst, West Sussex.
GU29 9AZ   Tel:01730 813169

EVOLVING THE ULTIMATE RAIL ENCYCLOPEDIA

www.middletonpress.co.uk   email:info@middletonpress.co.uk
A-0 906520   B-1 873793   C-1 901706   D-1 904474

OOP Out of Print at time of printing - Please check current availability   **BROCHURE AVAILABLE SHOWING NEW TITLES**

A
Abergavenny to Merthyr C 91 5
Aldgate & Stepney Tramways B 70 7
Allhallows - Branch Line to A 62 2
Alton - Branch Lines to A 11 8
Andover to Southampton A 82 7
Ascot - Branch Lines around A 64 9
Ashburton - Branch Line to B 95 2
Ashford - Steam to Eurostar B 67 7
Ashford to Dover A 48 7
Austrian Narrow Gauge D 04 7
Avonmouth - BL around D 42 X
B
Banbury to Birmingham D 27 6
Barking to Southend C 80 X
Barnet & Finchley Tramways B 93 6
Barry - Branch Lines around D 50 0
Basingstoke to Salisbury A 89 4
Bath Green Park to Bristol C 36 2
Bath to Evercreech Junction A 60 6
Bath Tramways B 86 3
Battle over Portsmouth 1940 A 29 0
Battle over Sussex 1940 A 79 7
Bedford to Wellingborough D 31 4
Betwixt Petersfield & Midhurst A 94 0
Blitz over Sussex 1941-42 B 35 9
Bodmin - Branch Lines around B 83 9
Bognor at War 1939-45 B 59 6
Bombers over Sussex 1943-45 B 51 0
Bournemouth & Poole Trys B 47 2 OOP
Bournemouth to Evercreech Jn A 46 0
Bournemouth to Weymouth A 57 6
Bournemouth Trolleybuses C 10 9
Bradford Trolleybuses D 19 5
Brecon to Neath D 43 8
Brecon to Newport D 16 0
Brickmaking in Sussex B 19 7
Brightons Tramways B 02 2
Brighton to Eastbourne A 16 9
Brighton to Worthing A 03 7
Bristols Tramways B 57 X
Bristol to Taunton D 03 9
Bromley South to Rochester B 23 5 OOP
Bude - Branch Line to B 29 4
Burnham to Evercreech Jn A 68 1
Burton & Ashby Tramways C 51 6
C
Camberwell & West Norwood Tys B 22 7
Cambridge to Ely C 55 1
Canterbury - Branch Lines around B 58 8
Caterham & Tattenham Corner B 25 1
Changing Midhurst C 15 X
Chard and Yeovil - BLs around C 30 3
Charing Cross to Dartford A 75 4
Charing Cross to Orpington A 96 7
Cheddar - Branch Line to B 90 1
Cheltenham to Andover C 43 5
Chesterfield Tramways D 37 3
Chesterfield Trolleybuses D 51 9
Chichester to Portsmouth A 14 2 OOP
Clapham & Streatham Tramways B 97 9
Clapham Junction - 50 yrs C 06 0
Clapham Junction to Beckenham Jn B 36 7
Clevedon & Portishead - BLs to D 18 7
Collectors Trains, Trolleys & Trams D 29 2
Cornwall Narrow Gauge D 56 X
Crawley to Littlehampton A 34 7
Cromer - Branch Lines around C 26 5
Croydons Tramways B 42 1
Croydons Trolleybuses B 73 1 OOP
Croydon to East Grinstead B 48 0
Crystal Palace (HL) & Catford Loop A 87 8
D
Darlington Trolleybuses D 33 0
Dartford to Sittingbourne B 34 0
Derby Tramways D 17 9
Derby Trolleybuses C 72 9
Derwent Valley - Branch Line to the D 06 3
Didcot to Banbury D 02 0
Didcot to Swindon C 84 2
Didcot to Winchester C 13 3
Douglas to Peel C 88 5
Douglas to Port Erin C 55 9
Douglas to Ramsey D 39 X
Dover's Tramways B 24 3
Dover to Ramsgate A 78 9
E
Ealing to Slough C 42 7

Eastbourne to Hastings A 27 4
East Cornwall Mineral Railways D 22 5
East Croydon to Three Bridges A 53 3
East Grinstead - Branch Lines to A 07 X
East Ham & West Ham Tramways B 52 9
East Kent Light Railway A 61 4
East London - Branch Lines of C 44 3
East London Line B 80 4
East Ridings Secret Resistance D 21 7
Edgware & Willesden Tramways C 18 4
Effingham Junction - BLs around A 74 6
Eltham & Woolwich Tramways B 74 X
Ely to Kings Lynn C 53 2
Ely to Norwich C 90 7
Embankment & Waterloo Tramways B 41 3
Enfield & Wood Green Trys C 03 6 OOP
Enfield Town & Palace Gates - BL to D 32 2
Epsom to Horsham A 30 4
Euston to Harrow & Wealdstone C 89 3
Exeter & Taunton Tramways B 32 4
Exeter to Barnstaple B 15 4
Exeter to Newton Abbot C 49 4
Exeter to Tavistock B 69 3
Exmouth - Branch Lines to B 00 6 OOP
F
Fairford - Branch Line to A 52 5
Falmouth, Helston & St. Ives - BL to C 74 5
Fareham to Salisbury A 67 3
Faversham to Dover B 05 7 OOP
Felixstowe & Aldeburgh - BL to D 20 9
Fenchurch Street to Barking C 20 6
Festiniog - 50 yrs of enterprise C 83 4
Festiniog in the Fifties B 68 5
Festiniog in the Sixties B 91 X
Finsbury Park to Alexandra Palace C 02 8
Frome to Bristol B 77 4
Fulwell - Trams, Trolleys & Buses D 11 X
G
Garraway Father & Son A 20 7 OOP
Gloucester to Bristol D 35 7
Gosport & Horndean Trys B 92 8 OOP
Gosport - Branch Lines around A 36 3
Great Yarmouth Tramways D 13 6
Greenwich & Dartford Tramways B 14 6 OOP
Guildford to Redhill A 63 0
H
Hammersmith & Hounslow Trys C 33 8
Hampshire Narrow Gauge D 36 5
Hampshire Waterways A 84 3 OOP
Hampstead & Highgate Tramways B 53 7
Harrow to Watford D 14 4
Hastings to Ashford A 37 1 OOP
Hastings Tramways B 18 9 OOP
Hastings Trolleybuses B 81 2 OOP
Hawkhurst - Branch Line to A 66 5
Hayling - Branch Line to A 12 6
Haywards Heath to Seaford A 28 2 OOP
Henley, Windsor & Marlow - BL to C 77 X
Hereford to Newport D 54 3
Hitchin to Peterborough D 07 1
Holborn & Finsbury Tramways B 79 0
Holborn Viaduct to Lewisham A 81 9
Horsham - Branch Lines to A 02 9
Huddersfield Trolleybuses C 92 3
Hull Tramways D60 8
Hull Trolleybuses D 24 1
Huntingdon - Branch Lines around A 93 2
I
Ilford & Barking Tramways B 61 8
Ilford to Shenfield C 97 4
Ilfracombe - Branch Line to B 21 9
Ilkeston & Glossop Tramways D 40 3
Industrial Rlys of the South East A 09 6
Ipswich to Saxmundham C 41 9/8 OOP
Ipswich Trolleybuses D 59 4
Isle of Wight Lines - 50 yrs C 12 5
K
Kent & East Sussex Waterways A 72 X
Kent Narrow Gauge C 45 1
Kingsbridge - Branch Line to C 98 2
Kingston & Hounslow Loops A 83 5
Kingston & Wimbledon Tramways B 56 1
Kingswear - Branch Line to C 17 6
L
Lambourn - Branch Line to C 70 2
Launceston & Princetown - BL to C 19 2
Lewisham & Catford Tramways B 26 X OOP
Lewisham to Dartford A 92 4

Lines around Wimbledon B 75 8
Liverpool Street to Chingford D 01 2
Liverpool Street to Ilford C 34 6
Liverpool Tramways - Eastern C 04 4
Liverpool Tramways - Northern C 46 X
Liverpool Tramways - Southern C 23 0
London Bridge to Addiscombe B 20 0 OOP
London Bridge to East Croydon A 58 4
London Chatham & Dover Railway A 88 6
London Termini - Past and Proposed D 00 4
London to Portsmouth Waterways B 43 X
Longmoor - Branch Lines to A 41 X
Looe - Branch Line to C 22 2
Lyme Regis - Branch Line to A 45 2
Lynton - Branch Line to B 04 9
M
Maidstone & Chatham Tramways B 40 5
Maidstone Trolleybuses C 00 1 OOP
March - Branch Lines around B 09 X
Margate & Ramsgate Tramways C 52 4
Marylebone to Rickmansworth D49 7
Midhurst - Branch Lines around A 49 5
Midhurst - Branch Lines to A 01 0 OOP
Military Defence of West Sussex A 23 1
Military Signals, South Coast C 54 0
Minehead - Branch Line to A 80 0
Mitcham Junction Lines B 01 4
Mitchell & company C 59 1
Moreton-in-Marsh to Worcester D 26 8
Moretonhampstead - Branch Line to C 27 3
N
Newbury to Westbury C 66 4
Newport - Branch Lines to A 26 6
Newquay - Branch Lines to C 71 0
Newton Abbot to Plymouth C 60 5
Northern France Narrow Gauge C 75 3
North East German Narrow Gauge D 44 6
North Kent Tramways B 44 8
North London Line B 94 4
North Woolwich - BLs around C 65 6
Norwich Tramways C 40 0
Nottinghamshire & Derbyshire Tramway
D 53 5
O
Orpington to Tonbridge B 03 0
Oxford to Moreton-in-Marsh D 15 2
P
Paddington to Ealing C 37 0
Paddington to Princes Risborough C 81 8
Padstow - Branch Line to B 54 5
Plymouth - BLs around B 98 7
Plymouth to St. Austell C 63 X
Porthmadog 1954-94 - BL around B 31 6
Porthmadog to Blaenau B 50 2 OOP
Portmadoc 1923-46 - BL around B 13 8
Portsmouths Tramways B 72 3 OOP
Portsmouth to Southampton A 31 2
Portsmouth Trolleybuses C 73 7
Princes Risborough - Branch Lines to D 05 5
Princes Risborough to Banbury C 85 0
R
Railways to Victory C 16 8/7 OOP
Reading to Basingstoke B 27 8
Reading to Didcot C 79 6
Reading to Guildford A 47 9 OOP
Reading Tramways B 87 1
Reading Trolleybuses C 05 2
Redhill to Ashford A 73 8
Return to Blaenau 1970-82 C 64 8
Roman Roads of Surrey C 61 3
Roman Roads of Sussex C 48 6
Romneyrail C 32 X
Ryde to Ventnor A 19 3
S
Salisbury to Westbury B 39 1
Salisbury to Yeovil B 06 5
Saxmundham to Yarmouth C 69 9
Saxony Narrow Gauge D 47 0
Seaton & Eastbourne T/Ws B 76 6 OOP
Seaton & Sidmouth - Branch Lines to A 95 9
Secret Sussex Resistance B 82 0
SECR Centenary album C 11 7
Selsey - Branch Line to A 04 5 OOP
Sheerness - Branch Lines around B 16 2
Shepherds Bush to Uxbridge T/Ws C 28 1
Shrewsbury - Branch Line to A 86 X
Sierra Leone Narrow Gauge D 28 4
Sittingbourne to Ramsgate A 90 8

Slough to Newbury C 56 7
Solent - Creeks, Crafts & Cargoes D
Southamptons Tramways B 33 2 OOP
Southampton to Bournemouth A 42 8
Southend-on-Sea Tramways B 28 6
Southern France Narrow Gauge C 4
Southwark & Deptford Tramways B
Southwold - Branch Line to A 15 0
South Eastern & Chatham Railways
South London Line B 46 4
South London Tramways 1903-33 D
St. Albans to Bedford D 08 X
St. Austell to Penzance C 67 2
St. Pancras to St. Albans C 78 8
Stamford Hill Tramways B 85 5
Steaming through Cornwall B 30 8
Steaming through Kent A 13 4 OOP
Steaming through the Isle of Wight A
Steaming through West Hants A 69 X
Stratford-upon-Avon to Cheltenham
Strood to Paddock Wood B 12 X
Surrey Home Guard C 57 5
Surrey Narrow Gauge C 87 7
Surrey Waterways A 51 7 OOP
Sussex Home Guard C 24 9
Sussex Narrow Gauge C 68 0
Sussex Shipping Sail, Steam & Moto
Swanley to Ashford B 45 6
Swindon to Bristol C 96 6
Swindon to Gloucester D46 2
Swindon to Newport D 30 6
Swiss Narrow Gauge C 94 X
T
Talyllyn - 50 years C 39 7
Taunton to Barnstaple B 60 X
Taunton to Exeter C 82 6
Tavistock to Plymouth B 88 X
Tees-side Trolleybuses D 58 6
Tenterden - Branch Line to A 21 5
Thanet's Tramways B 11 1 OOP
Three Bridges to Brighton A 35 5
Tilbury Loop C 86 9
Tiverton - Branch Lines around C 62
Tivetshall to Beccles D 41 1
Tonbridge to Hastings A 44 4
Torrington - Branch Lines to B 37 5
Tunbridge Wells - Branch Lines to A
Twickenham & Kingston Trys C 35 4
Two-Foot Gauge Survivors C 21 4 O
U
Upwell - Branch Line to B 64 2
V
Victoria & Lambeth Tramways B 49
Victoria to Bromley South A 98 3
Victoria to East Croydon A 40 1
Vivarais C 31 1
W
Walthamstow & Leyton Tramways B
Waltham Cross & Edmonton Trys C
Wandsworth & Battersea Tramways
Wantage - Branch Line to D 25 X
Wareham to Swanage - 50 yrs D 09 8
War on the Line A 10 X
War on the Line VIDEO + 88 0
Waterloo to Windsor A 54 1
Waterloo to Woking A 38 X OOP
Watford to Leighton Buzzard D 45 4
Wenford Bridge to Fowey C 09 5
Westbury to Bath B 55 3
Westbury to Taunton C 76 1
West Cornwall Mineral Railways D
West Croydon to Epsom B 08 1
West London - Branch Lines of C 50
West London Line B 84 7
West Sussex Waterways A 24 X
West Wiltshire - Branch Lines of C
Weymouth - Branch Lines around A
Willesden Junction to Richmond B 7
Wimbledon to Beckenham C 58 3
Wimbledon to Epsom B 62 6
Wimborne - Branch Lines around A
Wisbech - Branch Lines around C 0
Wisbech 1800-1901 C 93 1
Woking to Alton A 59 2
Woking to Portsmouth A 25 8
Woking to Southampton A 55 X
Woolwich & Dartford Trolleys B 66 9
Worcester to Hereford D 38 1
Worthing to Chichester A 06 1 OOP
Y
Yeovil - 50 yrs change C 38 9
Yeovil to Dorchester A 76 2
Yeovil to Exeter A 91 6